SHAKE

SHAKE

Joshua Beckman

WAVE BOOKS

Seattle • New York

Published by Wave Books
www.wavepoetry.com

Wave Books titles are distributed to the trade by
Consortium Book Sales and Distribution
1045 Westgate Drive, St. Paul, Minnesota 55114

Library of Congress Cataloging-in-Publication Data:
Beckman, Joshua, 1971–
  Shake / Joshua Beckman.— 1st ed.
     p. cm.
  ISBN 1-933517-04-2 (hardcover : alk. paper) — ISBN 1-933517-00-X (trade paper : alk. paper)
  I. Title.
  PS3552.E2839S53 2006
  811'.54—dc22

                    2005023694

Poems from this book first appeared in *Alaska Quarterly Review, American Letters and Commentary, Baffling Combustions, Conduit, Denver Quarterly, Fence, Insurance, jubilat, Knock, The Literary Review, Lyric, Now Culture, Poetry, Shade, Soft Target, Swerve* and *Verse*. The author wishes to thank the editors of these publications as well as his family and friends.

Cover art by Joshua Beckman
Designed and composed by J. Johnson
Printed in the United States of America

9 8 7 6 5 4 3 2 1

First Edition

Wave Books 002

CONTENTS

★ ★ ★

SHAKE

LET THE PEOPLE DIE

LET THE PEOPLE DIE

NEW HAVEN

SHAKE

* * *

Unslide the door,
uncap the lazy little coffee cup.
The pasty people must be part of the dinner.
And a city turns its incapacity in,
foolish city. She was naked
and her halo all crushed against
the pillow while she slept, but I
didn't care. Wake and totter.
Place a hand over your mouth,
a hand over another.
A killing pain, a bag all organized,
an inch of skin along your leg.
It's like they kept making babies
and stopped making baby whistles.
Doable, yes, but here they
teach us something different.
It's a battery. It's a garden.
The glass box in which the lettuce grew
was broken by nasty raccoons
and we turned the other cheek.
The sun does rise and melt the frost,
the frost in little drops does fill
the empty lettuce, and in this way
the world is truly nourished.
No incredible silence, no
intangible calorie, just
bad raccoon in a good world.
Just coverless table and

silent drape awaiting breakfast.
Imagine how mean people
can be in dreams, and how
kind sleeping seems later.

* * *

In the days of famous want
the people acted cruel and sweet
the music was boring and insightful
and if one found oneself in a well
the others would pull you from that well.
That is how it was. The countryside
unintelligible in its evaporation
and the people, their faces, full
and with nothing to do. One would
lie with the beloved and cheerless
and await the passing over
of smoke, such clouds, and
the endeavors of the day
would be discussed, the
anecdotal annunciations would
fill the spoons which earlier
had been filled with the humble
presentation of intangible thought.
We had been left. We had poured ribbons
in each other's bags. We had collapsed
beside each other's beds – the
calla lily floats above the table,
about the hands of certain people,
a glow. With you there in such
historic towns, I'm brought down.
We, at all times, have learned
to dance and to throw. We have
made gallant our enigmatic ways,
and when our teeth part or

when our lips open, we are doing
what we are born to do – our
bodies so unimportant amidst
the bodies of others, our memories
so well painted, our futures
so full of expensive shirts.
And the uncomfortableness
of watching someone's hand
cover the body of someone else.
It is history and it is money
and it is the ugly hats the women
you're always with want to wear,
it is the unacceptable swagger
of the iced, threading their way
through our life, and it is
the bridge, how you climb
atop it now and the waters
below you doing their stupid
repetitive thing, and the air
emptied of its sound, and the
shallow acts of others, and the fly
and the grass you will never see,
the constant emptying.
Carl once wrote the most horrible
poem, and I pinned it to my wall
and where is it now?
I empty myself of wit and begin,
and before long, a tow truck,
a snowstorm, the thought of him

going to California to make
other people miserable, the
thought again, the thought of
the sea, the unbecoming ways
of everyone, and other moments,
your red pants, your cradled purse,
the next man who will leave
his lover for you.

* * *

Everything's quiet,
everything in the world is quiet.
The smell of soap
and the afternoon are gone.
The subway's emptied out
and the subway tracks
displaying grayness
and the architectural grandeur
of an underground aqueduct.
People moving slowly away
from their personalities
and, I guess, into sleep.
I too, at one time, felt the elation of being a small drunken cog
in a giant destructive empire.
It means when you do nothing,
others may display that nothing in your name.
We may invent.
We may embrace personal decay.
We may, out of something we would like to call instinct,
shuffle together through an abandonment of practicality.
No one can explain even a little what's going down.
The stork in cosmic descension.
The born are born.
The live, live.
The ecstasy of your pantry.
When you returned with a tan
we loved you more.
We absolutely wanted you.
The powerful and how they think of uselessness.

The powerful and how they think of uselessness.
Jenny, after you left I became a bartender.
I was enamored with dark tortured women.
The world was birds, birds, bleachers and waves.
Break through and it's there.
A man who made films.
A shifting scale of useless ambition.
Women's shoes that when you touch them do nothing.
Women's shoes that when you touch them do nothing.

★ ★ ★

Death lasts
the thrifty nickel
destroyed my father
but who cares
if the boss gets in at six
you get in at quarter of
Rolling his cigarettes lefty impressed me
That month I had to stay in the basement
dragged me down
so I left for Deary
and who on earth am I telling this to
People of Deary gather round
my father's dying a Connecticut death
and you don't even know what that means
Picture the pigeons
contagion
and routine
sucking in the last
bit of air
you don't care
go back to your beautiful mountains
and your fucking potatoes
the dead man in the sun cannot be helped
and Idaho cried "Our ambulances are only for us."
and I saw the best minds of my generation
living in lofts
thinking they were the best minds of their generation
while the world hacked up tax breaks and jet fighters
"A true patriot kills himself when he's done with the wife and kids."
Listen, you little faggot, wipe the ants from your beard

———

and die without grace
die without pretension
die without knowledge
Aunt Mary's letters are charming
but they're not art
and to think that you know more than anyone else
is pathetically inconsistent with the idea that you know anything at all, dig?
And the Americans titter with glee,
heartless bunch
that we are
choking on our own individual retardations
while off in the distance
the potato king flies a flag bigger than the nightly news
above a lawn bigger than the nightly news
and the formal diamond of cheerleaders dismounts in the fading sunlight
on the side of a mountain and a thousand crazy pigeons
fly from behind Roosevelt High as in a dream
which is how everything happens
beautiful subtle and small
you're right
you sent me off to school
and they were teaching everyone hypnotism
so I let them teach me hypnotism
and look at me,
the birds disband when I say
the ants fall into formation
and every night I go to sleep thinking
"Tomorrow I will quit smoking"
and every morning I wake up
and ask for my coffee.

★　★　★

I saw them all walk through
with a promise pinned to each sprouted smile.
The saw, the guitar, the sweet blue pulse
of every eye. This is how
people are said to act,
but get yourself together
and I'll start in on another.
Did you ever see the lovely daisy
of your chest held to?
That's a crowd.
That's a crowd of the sincere and wantful.
That's the sound of a pink sweater
hitting the floor.
Always we will want
but next year I will take
your pretty palm into my pants
and the Flanagan Family Singers
will pipe up with their only aloofness
and we will sing along
we will take each single sound
and leave it inside you
for there you are, afraid again
falling over every memory on your way
back from the bathroom.
Ugly people cover themselves in smoke,
and I'm one of them.
Countries fill their countrysides
with sheep so that their countrysides
can be nibbled upon – everyone's trying.

But you're at home jumpstarting each pore that opens.
Did I ever tell you how, when I was young,
I was the biggest doer,
all fathom and future,
pretending to understand?
Well, that's who you're sleeping with darling,
that's who stares into your eyes waiting again tonight.
Soon a place.
Soon a little open place.
And if you want to I want to too.
Swing over the sleeping earth
and fuck at will.

★　★　★

Epic endangerment of the heart
which is broken, of the soul
which is broken, of the cracked
indistinguishable persona
which is cracked and broken,
everyone wanting, everyone falling asleep
and to everyone who is cracked,
no sneakers can help you,
not their rubber, not their rubber,
not a knowledge of smallness or
wish to be covered. It is
callous to say there are a thousand
spotted owls and only one of me.
Maybe it's stupid to say such things
about extinction. Birds were falling
from the sky and this pornographer
I know was running around talking
about an angle I don't feel comfortable
mentioning. Maybe in a way I'm a
prude, and he says you know people
they're people. A Polish couple precise
with their memory and a junkie
with a tiny bit of etiquette. I fell
asleep on the pasalla. I was weak
taking off. Someone put my loafers
to the side, and the waves, only the wealthy
can afford such waves. Cuban cigars. You know,
some of the greatest men never had vacations.
I wrote PASCAL IN CANCUN. A boring book,

———

I admit, but that part where the girls
start rocking their heads back and forth.
That part where the sun just washes
over her forehead, and then a cheek
and then another and then the first again, etc.
That's all I cared about, but explain that
to a publisher. One rocky sea and the water
just splashes out of its glass. "Fantastic."
"Fantastic." Do it again cry the children.
I'm cracked. I'm done. I'm as a bell. I'm
aboard these rubber sneakers bound for destruction.
So, my little ones, next time you see me
coming by, scream out "die" "die" "die"
then you'll have fantastic.

★ ★ ★

Raise the flag of sexual pretense up.

The old wanted wind.

The young wanted something different
cruising through them.
I wanted an end to all distinctions –

ie: nude surfing is not something new

ie: the French have never been better lovers

ie: try, try, a racket of harshness beat you into a frenzy and as your moaning
filled the hostel, everyone encumbered by the foreignness of your song, she,
some three blocks away, leaned over a sailboat, a glass of wine, her pretty
hands, the smell of sunscreen makes me want to have already fucked this
afternoon, and run away with her wine, and her so happy to be rid of my
ugliness and me so happy to be rid of her subtleness, and we'll just hide this
regret under a pile of wet panties and come back to it later.

Every sailboat has a waterfall
Every slight attraction's desperate call

You know the inconspicuousness of your shorts
and I know it too
When they dump us out onto the floor lets beat the crap out of each other
until the cameraman starts sweating

and then let's smoke cigarettes

and then let's take pictures
and then run away
and find a guy with better posture

you were good to stay,
I know you love tall lanky men
but this is an experience and
that's why you decided to visit our city in the first place

The neighbors are cooking,
can you hear them cooking?

The neighbors are singing,
can you hear them singing?

If, before you head back, I run out to the store and buy you two very white
tennis socks, will, in that little naked morning you're bound to have soon,
you put on these socks?

The tiny scars
on your ivory feet

K Swiss K Swiss
Only I want to make them.

* * *

Beautiful rounded earth
we accept so your fluorescence,
the night coming into the town
in each person's heart, the soulful
advance over water our airplanes make,
the darkness that is water around them,
that we might be in equal sleep with others
and so to see the world as we have made it.
Teri, this poem is for you. The omelette was
great, I like to get high and talk about children.
The most optimistic version of architecture is
following this amazing chain of friends into
the world and helping them dawdle there,
but it's just not how it is. How it is
is people like blueberries so they climb mountains,
people like snowstorms so you move north,
people like people so they invite them
behind the restaurant to get high.
As I sit here in my low-flying plane
I think about all the effective coffee
and I think about the wonderful drawing
a town makes without knowing.
It is night, and even in brutal countries
like our own, the human beast belongs first
to friendship. Later fields. Later hills and dales.
Later square and unit, rent and sublet.
My America is still one overrun with gentle preference
and able give. All week a friendly thorough want
kept washing over me – a hamburger, a lecture,

a getting off the phone, that I might some day be a
painter (still), spending money, Dave, the girl
at the Strand, Franz Kline, John reminding me
that some people work way harder than I do.
Above the world we fly. In Pennsylvania we retire.
The best part of the story about the house in the woods
and the dirt road and the bar is the house in the woods
the dirt road and the bar, and that your vacation will come
(may it come soon). Air and leaves, a stream.
Later I will tell you about my neighbor and how
she gave me a dime off my soda – how stupid with sugar
and temperate elevation I was, and other things.
That people, all at once, can be kind and thoughtful.

★ ★ ★

Headlights in daylight.
Our first exchange was Arizona crossing California.
Pulling out the water, floating down the river,
whistling, disappointed and riverless.
Not caring for a new motorcycle and walking all the way back.
A bad meal at the house (they closed and wanted to go home)
and we wanted to go home and be with no one,
which turned out to be "not so good."
Unable to write or return to the bar.
God knows how I will explain this in forty years.
How empty I was and the place was
and we were like each other, which was good.
But it was the New Age with love and one consciousness.
It was the new way and we were not so comfortable with it yet.
But out of a hope for kindness we stopped in the garden
and dropped our guns and cigarettes.
The lizards ran out of the way and the garden grew tobacco.
The spirit of the place was unchanged by thousands of people moving there,
living there and leaving.
How can that be?
Lizard lizard go away, come again some other day.
I am fashioning the world's largest sand garden, for pride,
for the respect of my family,
and for contemplation's sake.
The moon will rise over it.
The old will crease it with their cadillacs.
The lizards, at night, will be entertained by my effort.
I will miss work and reproduce the feeling of driving alone.
I will rake without music.

I will ignore the military, their planes passing, and they will ignore me.
I will dream of romance and become disenchanted.
I will leave despite leaving the job unfinished.
I will sell the land to a family of four.
They will leave before leaving it to their children.
All will reach an age and then die at that age.

★ ★ ★

The swans were swimming in a pool in the park.
Stephanie was dead. Everyone was married,
and brought to see the swans and again to see the swans.
The city was finite and eternal. We were having dinner.
He was trying to tell me and not knowing how to put it.
I had become someone else, not the person we wanted me to be.
Dinner came. The day ended. Every sentence was punctuated perfectly.
I kept being with people and people kept not being right.
I was wrong, that was for certain. All I wanted was to write
a sentence so long even I couldn't finish it. But I couldn't.
Language was not my greatest asset and that was a problem.
Years passed. Can you say that in a poem. Years passed,
and someone without wanting to had gone away a dozen times or more.
They didn't hate their jobs. They didn't love their jobs.
I thought we were doing okay and it was wrong.
In the time that elapsed a dozen people came and went.
Knowing you should do anything would be better.
New cars hellish because of the debt they cause you
are only worth it when you crash them into telephone poles
and call from the police station stupid with your life
being treated like something you found.
The angels appeared for him and he embraced them.
Actually, the angels appeared in his life simply due to the fact
that he asked them to come and they came and what sort of lesson
should this teach us and what sort of lesson are we asking for these days,
to be our only lesson and is not. Why would you want angels.
That is the worst and most upsetting question.
Why would you not?
Again, questions are not for this sort of state.

———

Statements and curses.
I sentence you to die and the angel died.
That was appropriate.

★ ★ ★

Final poem for the gently sifting public begins on the streets,
the police turning corners, the people exact in their gaits,
the all-knowing god existent in minds everywhere.
The shower running because I am sitting on the floor with a joint,
in my small book there is a story about this.
The crude protectiveness of one mistaken person seems too much.
The floor is rented.
The shower is rented.
The water is purchased almost unintentionally.
It is not memory that treats you this way,
you should know that by now.
Why is there no music in the house.
Why have you begun to set a record for dreariness,
may I ask you that.
Why can't the chevrolet seem like a swan
when that is what I want.
Surrealism is old, so everyone should get some.
Why did the water disappear before the swan arrived.
Why did the swan disappear before the swan arrived.
Why won't the poem write itself as I drift into the shower,
as I levitate above the yoga mat,
as I perform the perfect pose upon the yoga mat.
I ask little of the passing hand of mental celebrity.
I am not greedy.
I will do what I am told.
I will not attempt to create the eucalyptus tree
or steal the lines of other poets.
Oh Peter, I stole a tree from your poem
and now it is gone, and you at home

and me without your number.
Is it me crashing into the typewriter as waves?
Is it me exploding with letters that mean nothing?
Is it me moving about the city like a police car
not looking for trouble and not finding it?
No, it is the drink.
It is the days.
No, it is the passing.
Bakersfield, California cried out
and I said something like
"I cannot hear you above the crashing defense
of heaven and hell that goes on here."
We were at the center of unimportant things that made noise.
They informed us of nothing.
If we were swept up in the high school students
going to get high, and we went with them to get high,
and they allowed us that when we brought the stuff,
and if they didn't knock us into the river,
and if they didn't secretly hate us,
and if they didn't notice our brains fighting,
and if they were content and did not disown us for this fighting,
and if they secretly had wishes unrelated to us in our presence,
and if we babbled unmindfully and they said
"that dude is fucked up" so we could hear,
and if no one cared how we kept looking at them,
how our thoughts swirled around them,
and if they didn't push us in the river,
but thought that is how you get when you get like this.
We would ask to pass the oxygen,

we would watch them leave,
we would say look out for the police,
they are moving in a grid,
they are carried by something greater than themselves,
they are in control of their cars but their cars are in control,
and this is not a paradox,
they are more afraid of you than you are of them,
they would say we know, fuck them,
and we would know what they meant,
that they meant no harm.

LET THE PEOPLE DIE

A rake in the garden. The garden
is rotting. The house and the yard.
The garden is rotting. A rake in
the pond. The pond and the swimming.
The house and the yard, the garden
and pond. Outside the neighbors
a rake in the garden. The rake,
it is rotting. The yard and the pond.
Out past the neighbors a woman is
walking. Out past the neighbors
a rake in the yard. The pond and
the swimming. The woman is walking.
The rake in the garden. The rake
in the yard. Out past the neighbors.

In the blue pond a flame. I'm sorry,
I've been smoking again. The pond
reached the woods and stopped. It will
have its life there. Rotten wood or
a wood that is overgrown. Lay down.
The deer. I've been smoking again.
It happens naturally. The pond covers
over. The leaves. The legs of a mammal.
Your letter arrived and sat there. It will
have its life there. I know what you
mean. Walking in the overgrown
wood. A pond there. I know what
you mean. Lay down there. I've been
walking around and will stop there.

The canals. The liquor coming through
the straw. The canals the land and
the bridge and the landing by the bridge
destroyed. The liquor. The little anger
growing inside the friends. The canal.
The pile of wood up against the bank.
The liquor. The friends. A little
anger growing inside them. The canal.
The jets. The wood in piles along
the bank. The dead. The jets. Liquor
through a straw. Speaking. A little anger
grows inside them. The jets. The dead.
The bank. The sky. The friends. The jets.
The dead. A little anger grows inside them.

That's the worst way. The thin tree. The
brick and its acceptance of light. The brick
and its continued darkness. Now, in the
wind, there's no way to explain. The room.
It is comfortable. A quiet towel sits in the
windowsill. The hallway. Let me explain.
It's the worst way. The hallway. Outside,
the light gives itself to the brick and the brick
accepts the light. The wind told me this.
I'm okay. A small towel flaps in the window.
The hallway. Yesterday, I'd say two days.
There is no way to explain. The brick's
acceptance of light and light giving itself to
the brick. The wind. There's no way to explain.

There upon your utter pale and lovely future
the sun. You light up. Something electric
lands beside you. You're right. The flags.
The anxious crisscrossing. Electric light
and the glass. Just lather up in sunscreen
and disappear. This hornet was made by
the French and left here to die. Glass is
impossibly versatile. I look at it. I crisscross
in some inventive personal way. The buttons.
A reflection in the buttons. The sand. A reflection
in the sand. A French hornet reflecting.
Just lather up in sunscreen and disappear.
You're right. It's something about the light.
A crisscrossing in the sand. The sun.

———

The dead girl by the beautiful Bartlett.
I'm sad. I make horrible sentences.
A woman alone in the park waves. The water.
The dead girl by the beautiful Bartlett.
Put down the cell phone. I'm sad. The waves.
The horrible staring. A woman alone
in the park. Waves. The leaves. Leaves
alone in the park. I'm staring. The
dead girl by the beautiful Bartlett. I'm sad.
Put down your cell phone. A wave.
The sad girl alone in the park. Leaves.
Put down your cell phone. The Bartlett.
The staring. A leaf alone in the horrible
leaves. The dead girl. The staring.

Desperate bastards breaking bottles
over the heads of other desperate bastards.
A bloody cut crawls through the skin.
Truly. Nothing is more unruly than your lethargy.
Bastards beating bastards in the beautiful sunlight.
Look, I crawled through your skin to watch
the fight. Sit quietly. Wait patiently. Sobriety
forgot just what it thought of me. Desperate bastards
break bottles over the sunny heads of the now hollowed out.
Unsteady is your lethargy. A bottle bobbed
its way toward me. Bastards vying for a cut to
crawl through. Wait patiently. Sunlight's bloody break
upon the desperate sea. Sobriety, sobriety –
Now we're hollowed out by constancy.

Really. The laughing at children. The dallying.
I have smoked my way down to the
dreadful bottom, and it's rather pleasant here.
A brief white light. Little puddles of reflective
water. See. The sky within water and the water
without the sky. Really. The children are
laughing. It's pleasant. The slow quake. The
light. The sky reflected in water where there
is no sky. Really. It's quite pleasant. A picture
here. Really. The puddles. The quiet
here. The sense that you will walk through
here presently, though you are not here.
Really. I've smoked my way down to the
dreadful bottom, and it's rather pleasant here.

The thirst of the crowd. We laid the surfer down.
The child and the child. Come look what I have found.
Our country is in disgraceful times and you bring
this around. The thirst of the crowd. Another dead thing
on the ground. A body. The dimness and the broken board.
The display of a body. The child and the child.
Come look what I have found. Lay the surfer down.
Another dead thing on the ground, and you
brought this around. The child and the child.
Come look what I have found. A surfer there upon
the ground. The child and the child. Far away a little
sound. Come look what I have found. The crowd
and the crowd. The surfer laid out on the ground.
In the disgraceful dimness of our country, your body.

———

The cops calling and a crowd filling the parking lot.
Determination. An empty season. I'm leaving. I'm moving
home. Mystical and dramatic are the works now beginning.
Determination. The cops are calling. You twist about in
the day's degenerative passing. Nothing. Nothing
but the sound of the crackhead's sickly wailing.
A degenerative passing of the day. The cops calling.
There at home nothing moving. Mystical and dramatic.
The empty season beginning. The crackhead singing. There
and twisting. I lost my shoes, but I have my walkman. There.
Nothing new but a season leaving. Dramatic and determined.
I'm moving. The day's degenerative passing. A quiet
wailing from the crowd's gathering. The day filling and twisting.
Emptying. I'm moving home. The day is passing.

The birds know. The wind knows. Call me. I'm always
in the same place watching the same thing. The sound of
water, of wind, of flags, of the birds' deserved babies
crying for rain. The birds know. Translucent is the wallet
that holds the money on its way. Children stop. Pilgrims
stop. Tugboats drift. The wind knows. I'm always in the
same place watching the same thing. You know. The blue bridge
opening for no one. The water knows. A translucent wallet
filled with water. Flags flapping at the sign of water. We
know. We start singing at the sight of the translucent wallet
holding water. It's singing. It knows. It's always in
the same place watching the same thing. The blue bridge
opening for no one. The rain on its way to a wallet of water.
The birds know. Always the same place, the same thing.

The world. I don't know. We sink. We
are awkward. We lean. We fall into doors
and we sink into those doors. The world.
I am dressed as one who leans into
one who is bigger than himself. The world.
I don't know. To be next to you dear
brother. I am positioned as the one
who leans into the one bigger than himself.
The world. The world. The party was horrible.
Falling out into the dark walkway or only
sinking into the evening. I don't know.
Doors are leaning up against other doors
and it is awkward. We sink. We lean. We are
as one leaned up next to one who is bigger.

A death mask floating on the floral ocean.
Why did he do that. Why, when there are
tiny leaves to be trampled by tiny birds.
Spiders unequalled in their smallness and
$1 for a soda seems like a lot, but $100
for 100 sodas does not. It's hot. A
death mask floats on the floral ocean.
Why, when tiny birds, tiny leaves, did he
do that. The victory of fashion over weather.
The victory of heat over sensibility.
The victory of those who litter over
the earth, which I love. A death
mask floating on the floral ocean.
Fliers fill the space between buildings.

I like your handsome drugs. Your pleasant
drugs. Your frozen fingernails. Your painted
fingernails. That man screamed out, "The
karate chop of love," before tackling that woman.
The breeze. Your sort of quiet happy voices.
The karate chop of love. Your handsome drugs.
If you, in all your sexiness, could just bring that
over here. A barrel of fried chicken. That girl
named Katie. A birthday party. Yeah. I go
running in, all ready to show everyone the
karate chop of love. And that girl named Katie.
A barrel of chicken. The breeze. This
birthday party is fucked without the karate
chop of love. Your handsome drugs.

I'm happy here. The sun, the hot and masculine sun.
The light crossing the skin and the shoes sitting
nearly still in the sun. The day was ending,
but someone could describe it better. The gray light.
The gray light across the floor, the shoes, the hot sun.
The yellow hot sun. I'm here. I'm happy here.
I'm here. I'm asleep in the happy face of the sun,
the white face of the sun. A glare. A glare.
But someone could describe it better. Sitting
there. The sun. The hot and masculine sun.
The gray light across the floor. Nearly still. Just
sitting there. The light crossing the skin and the shoes.
The light crossing you as you are sitting there.
I'm happy here. The gray face of the sun is here. A glare.

In Latin there is a saying. Neither the tent
nor the description of the tent. Neither the sun
nor the description of the sun. You sit there
soaked in your little illusion. It's hot. We put you
down and forgot. The sun, the description
of the sun. The tent, the description of the tent.
A sort of false floral air filled the tent. There
is a saying in Latin. The tent left alone. The air
left alone. The description of the sun left
to beat down upon the empty tent. A floral air
surrounds you. The sun surrounds you.
A sort of bath laid down upon you. Upon
the empty tent. In Latin there is a saying.
Neither the tent nor the description of the tent.

The ants in reference to the already dead.
This: they crawl. They eat. They die.
People move across the dunes. Watch them
move across the dunes. They should have
built the apartment better. They should have
tried convincing each other. They crawl.
They eat. They burn. The already dead.
The dunes. Someone quietly closed
the apartment. It should have been built
better. It should have been covered over.
It's already clean, so what do you think.
This: empty the hallway of everything.
Wash the windows. Sweep whatever dirt
there is out of the way. Open it up for the already
dead. Soon our friends return from the dunes.

Here, in the marijuana forest, the sun god
has collapsed. The lungs have collapsed.
The police are asleep on the beach, which is
in the middle of the forest, which means
the police are lying down in the middle of
the forest, which means sweet prejudice
of the wingéd firefly opens inside you.
Watch from your perch in the marijuana forest.
The sun god. The fluttering around of the sun god.
The guns going off. The smile of the firefly
who loves the beach, who loves the forest,
who loves the little pool in which the policemen bathe.
By which the policemen sleep. A pile of guns.
A brief collapse of the lungs.

We have us here again in no good sort. The sly
and the mythic make a horrible cocktail.
The bartender hates me. She hates the dark,
the quiet, the sordid lounge. I joined
this club to learn about billiards, and that's it.
Crisscrossing the hall like a horrible bartender
looking for someone to spill a drink on.
The sly anecdote versus the mythic anecdote.
We have us here again in no good sort.
A quiet descends on the sordid lounge.
I joined this club to learn about billiards
and that's it. The cue ball, descendant of a
mythic cue ball. The eight ball, descendant of a
sly eight ball. We have us here again in no good sort.

Modest disease of the desperate Pole.
Children do not end up like her. Mothers are
to advice as blackbirds are to blackbirds.
Selfish and folded up on the corner. Selfish
and alone in the corner. It is her I want to
share this little cigarette with. My philosophy is
how horrible it is to wake up in the morning. How
horrible to find utensils covered in moonlight, to
find her curled in the corner, there in the moonlight.
To squeeze myself past the modest cabinet. Past the
dread Pole dead in the apartment. Her indulgence. Look
how mothers touch mothers and all hear out the window,
there's a dead drunk there in the apartment. Blackbirds are
blackbirds. Alone in the corner dying of moonlight.

All this horrible conquering in the name of Christianity.
I mean dating. I mean, one of us keeps going and that's not
nearly enough. All this terrible swimming, I mean sipping.
The soup in its horrible hotness. I came in here because
in here it's air-conditioned. I don't care what I eat.
All this horrible conquering in the name of nourishment.
I mean, I'm serious about politics and I'm serious about
all sorts of stuff, but I'm hot. The sun and how it keeps
horribly conquering in the name of nourishment. I mean,
I'm serious about the Christians. I mean, if I had any sense
that America believed in banjos, I'd pick somewhere else.
It's all this horrible conquering and the heat and the way
a little song plays inside you and the Christians whipping you
with their horrible heated debate. I mean politics. A dating.

A brief blaze on the pavement. A slow drunk with
a dark towel. I don't want to tell jokes, I want to
win the lottery. I subscribed to the new, not impractical
way of being, the inconspicuous, the incomplete.
A healthy stare and the skin which darkens and
the evening. A joke and you can kiss that seven hundred
dollars goodbye. I'm wrong. She's sitting downstairs.
A flower waits in the pool which is my intoxication.
A man walks into a bar. Seven hundred dollars later.
A blaze on the pavement. A darkened evening.
The skin. I'm wrong. She sits downstairs.
A healthy stare and the skin. A joke. I'm wrong.
A slow drunk. A dark towel waving in the evening.
Seven hundred dollars. A new, not impractical way of being.

Let the people die. The mysterious doctor. The blonde boy
bouncing around. Once you've broken town you're lost.
Let the people die. In the sun. Beneath the sun.
The mysterious doctor. The death of the brother.
The blonde boy. The blonde boy. And no one breaks town.
The children bouncing around. The pace of the slow sun,
the heat of the slow sun, and the weight of the slow sun.
Let the people die. The blonde boy. The mysterious doctor.
Hide. Hide and watch the blonde boy bouncing in the
mysterious sun. We're old. The sun, which travels
slowly, and the heat and the slow pace. The doctor,
the mysterious doctor. Dead in the corner. The running
around and bouncing of the blonde boy. Let them die.
The weight of the slow sun. Once you've broken town you're done.

Minute by minute we move toward the restoration.
What home. What borough have you holed up in.
Where, when it goes like this, are the gone, are
the going. Sometimes, often, you walk up to the
wall and you begin work on the wall, you're gone.
That's good. The restoration. Minute by minute.
My advice to you is this: don't listen, don't write down
what you hear, don't make a list, don't post the list.
You're gone. Minute by minute. The restoration,
covered in white, the standing wall. Staring. You
listen to something and a little bit later you walk
to the wall. In just a minute the wall is removed.
Some paint dripping and my advice to you is this:
Don't write down what you hear, don't listen.

A light puff of smoke in the warm air.
Descending and ascending. Off with the flowers
which were bought for you. The air knowing
everything. Get on your plane. My country
is big enough for me. And yours for you.
A light puff of smoke in the warm air.
Descending and ascending, no matter.
The workday for the worker, the paycheck etc.
The flowers which were bought for you.
The country. A puff of smoke. The heat,
lightening, the heat, lightening, the heat,
lightening, the heat. No matter. A puff of
smoke. A light puff of smoke in the warm
air. Nothing I'll ever say in your ear.

NEW HAVEN

* * *

They, lost, and to the
touch of one another do go
and to say such things
in the grass plain of day
gone long – to be comfortable
or to lay there ruining one's clothes
and in the air above the growing lawn
a bell reflects itself in sound
and asks – what will will leave you
this? – to touch and at once
to be touched. Easy again blows
the warm wind and we bend to it
as does the grass, but we are wanting.

★ ★ ★

Lying in bed I think about you,
your ugly empty airless apartment
and your eyes. It's noon, and tired
I look into the rest of the awake day
incapable of even awe, just
a presence of particle and wave,
just that closed and deliberate
human observance. Your thin fingers
and the dissolution of all ability. Lay
open now to only me that white body,
and I will, as the awkward butterfly,
land quietly upon you. A grace and
staying. A sight and ease. A spell
entangled. A span. I am inside you.
And so both projected, we are now
part of a garden, that is part of a
landscape, that is part of a world
that no one believes in.

★ ★ ★

Now begins our immaculate summer
or the clutter of what tunes itself near the truth
or they have made glasses just for me (gloomy things)
or her hand there on my chest (the street of champions)
or the chorus of taught and clumsy common quality
we have made ourselves unable to share. See, Vivian,
the whole world's gone typical, crying,
the bed's now set, the sun the same (snow) and you
kept painting (so rather studious) and for me,
remember, everything's fine, I think of her
universal and divine. She has a patio too, proud,
and in stillness one beautiful thing is brought forward
after another, and refused. Leisurely and pleased
I go. To collect of things is all I ever know.

* * *

In heaven there'll be umbrellas for children (their size).
Matt said that and the coordination of each thing
to its other is not some game but harmonics (as promised)
and the best version of blue outlives all others (the berry)
and there is a stillness given to rain which has nowhere to fall
(as after the music has ended and the vibration that architecture
has learned to embrace, it embraces and continues always to embrace)
or, I have a little music box I think too much about. And as for us
who are incompatible with our surroundings, we must pace ourselves
as the lovely raindrops in heaven, of which Matt so suredly spoke,

– cups of varied fullness –

and an untempered deflection about us continued to deflect and onward
to deflect. Space was made. Everything else was made to move through it.

★ ★ ★

On the contrary, he was astounded
to discover it was another, the horse
pulling the carriage through the dandelions
and watching them fold over

the weary plaintive whistling
of a lookout over birds

or as he kept saying, the moonlight
shining down, the lamplight shining down

the boat splashing through the garden
the town speaking to the stranger

another fearsome landscape
of beautiful shadows just shaking there,
the dream of which is to be seen

or again to be touched
on the cheek – s'étant
endormi doucement –
and inlaid in the cabinet,
shells, the ocean, the piper
piping above the bushes

as palms as groves as plans
as charm as safety as danger –
and will you ask again
"What's that?"

———

Sur le fleur, sur le fleur,
wrapped in a blissful dream
the moonlight shines down
brightly –

but I don't really know that
I just read it in a book.

★   ★   ★

Damage control of the fifth façade.
The buses kept running and flattened
by the fast that flowed through you,
threw another leaf, leaf into the air,
air into the pocket of blood
that promises to stop itself
from pumping, and pretty are the
accounts of our actions after
we have acted, pretty the list
of names and trifling judgments
I carried around with some forsaken wherewithal
and I crept through the grass so
covered in leaves that my legs
shook and those about me who seemed
poisoned did not die and those about me
one living overtook, the shake which
shakes us down is sung again aloud –
lackluster is the unnatural horrible
wrenching of that which works but does
not give, of that which takes, continues
always to take.

*   *   *

Again the flat world of borrowed things
and the banging of everything that is heavy
into everything else and the cosmos
of the unfeeling is, sadly, just as full
and seeing that is no better
than seeing anything else

                 or the dove crept into its damp
                 little hole or

I know how they treated you
and I can do nothing about it

* * *

A frieze and the empty system of everyone,
the water they live in, the dust they live in,
the horizon they wake to – did you hear
the voice unchanged, glassy, the want left alone,
the disposition of that want and the stone
unstared at by the sky – to be wrong
and to ignore what is good, to drift
as we without feelings into the bar and later
to leave – I have fucked the brains out of
every incandescent virtue I met, and look
where it got me – a whiskey sticky on my feet,
a senseless filling of the taxi with distant you,
a hopeless corruption of giving up keeping everyone
by the phone, so far from the beautiful.
There are people who can never be made happy
and there is a specific psychology for every lack.
By day I see the sparrows. By night I see
the bats. Beautiful to go and get what you want.
Wicked to sit back and watch others do it.

★　★　★

So to not be heard
it's him, for here to lay
down what one has made,
to watch the lovely drop on it
displayed – to make of something
something – to be done –
your voice is now that silent noise
we look – such is the fallen
ceiling, such is the constant pool –
your lights, when you spin your wheels,
the recession of memory until it is that drop or less
and the condensation we've come to bless
so as to make it certain and gone
of the mind
it has been said: its inabilities
are most interesting – that a square foot
of air cannot be filled with both
a bicycle and the sound of a bird,
that to lay in the grass and
await the falling leaves is only one thing,
though there be heat, though there be light,
though, elsewhere, there be her
continuing on with her life.

* ★ ★

Beautiful arbitrary reflexivity (the night).
A fat baby smiling from its bucket (the day).
Before the room gets too small, let me remind you
that everyone with a window already jumped.
Our point is assertion, not seduction,
but this will do. Here, take what I wrote
and as I ride away on the pulled-apart bicycle
the bitter dog will jump out of the mailbox
and the belly, detained by the shirt,
as Chekhov his nostalgic interpreters,
will fall out into the big world.
In German we will say
the word for sample is "ein exemplar"
and then run away – drink your coffee
and rue the day. When you return,
explain every humorous thing you can
about misinterpretation,
– an awkward smile, a boat for a candle –
I spent years preparing and then my feet began
to pound, I felt faint. In the most comforting way
you stood there behind me. I thought it then
and I think it even now: A weak woman
will never make you happy.

*   *   *

Of or to be in that light, to hide again
where the insects crawl, where the animals cower
and sleep, where the children grow bigger.
It's a drag to be alone everywhere,
you going through my stuff
me tired
the world acting pathetically mystic.
Let's wash our faces
and get back in bed.
The cats will come in
and you might right now or in the future
just start to feel things –
that the neighbors are fine
that fidgeting is not a sign of weakness
that the fan is ill-used by the sink
which reflects it
that music is beyond you in the best possible way,
you are pleased when the room cools down
you are pleased when your body sinks into that aloneness
and instead of having anyone
you can have dreams of anyone
you can accept for now this place
as a place you remember.
But the world betrays us all with its existence
and you especially with its continuity,
and some of us never had to hear a thing
upon some of us a spell was cast
each time we left the town

If you leave we will change
If you leave we will change
If you leave we will change

and I believed it.
Asleep, I took its magic in,
and before my life was that far along
I thought, "Here is where you are,
and there is where you will never go."
So place another silken slip upon your dreams
and accept that that is exactly what they are.

★ ★ ★

Kneeling by the prayer wheel
I saw it again

                    3 follows 2
                    2 follows 1

        and how best not to hurt anyone's feelings

The spinning of plates on poles
or the levitation of anything over a hand

or a song for which
we must help others
with their needs

                        or to have escaped a week ago
by raft – the beard, the equation of rations – The sun
and everyone back home carries on, for this is
how it is promised to be and so, how it is

        and from there the kicked-in center

of the sea squealed at our arrival
the centuries
and then the shoulder
and then the backseat driver
and then affixed to the screen

        and to each other, and then again

———

with the blue world before us, unfearful, as
around everyone the axe dance continues

for we get dressed and we pray and
some thus far too lovely
and this way (and this way
are done again) the pale, passed
on – thy directive and ways

Hold me so, and let me
explain what I have learned

The craft rocked in the weakening waves,
our catch drying upon it, and us in one
open cove after another

and what I saw from down there was a growing bright in others,
one at a time

to know and to come to know

* * *

This is what's been done to flesh
the quill and the book and the
indiscretion of stone upon which
a little drop of gold does fall,
the cry of a pigeon or moan
of the folded over father, and
beneath these drapéd mysteries
the wine does spill upon the dog
the dog does sit in the corner
curing itself of this indifference
and the bar of light does illumine
such dust as has been brought
into upheaval with only your
untidy waking – the covers under
your chin:

                pull

and in the distant river
they are listening, cut grass
blown through the window and
why music and the absorbency
of such concrete as has distilled
the discordance of the neighborhood
and has left "through the music
he sweetly displays" an empty field
of lost balloons rolling into streets
as have, in other times, volcanoes
covered such singers as do justice

to the cosmic tops they had seen through
their equally majestic windows, the mint
leaf touched the lip, the regular
resurrection of those empty spaces
that result from banishment,
the ladder leaned against a tree,
Dear Margaret, I, in such
constant envious refrain as does inform
most open speech, do extend and my
flower does tap your halo – how it spins
now surrounded by such baggèd peoples
as only Florida can offer. I have set
your aura a runnin and from it (its sun)
I gather light. This, you see,
is our domestic partnership – the
conclusion of each well-attached earring
and fragrant misunderstanding, the chorus
of the barbaric calling, while here in the meeting
I'm passed this note:

>Dismal are we who love only recognition
>Now hand me the saber.

Which I did.

1:00 pm   Behind curtain
               baby kissing mother

1:05 pm   Clouds cover mountains

1:10 pm   Ribbons in patterns descending

1:20 pm   Tragic event of saber and table

The flesh. In time you will learn to look
at everything. In time you will learn to
touch everything. In time you will learn
to clothe everything. In time you will
learn to eat everything. In time you will
learn to say of everything that it has
been seen, that it has been touched, that
it has been killed, that it has been eaten.
Bloodied are our hours, in reflection,
the knuckle and the finger and the paper.
The shoulder. At dusk I did slip from the town,
the baby under my wing. Now to the water,
where what I have done will be reflected on later.

* * *

I take a turn toward the map
and see how it is struck again with light,
its talents and deep beliefs cleaning and reflecting
as anything noticed scampering across the floor
can sit quite easily in memory for hours
promising to return to another open garden of goodness
in a minute, but thinking instead,
take one's task in stride
know what is to be told and what is to be kept to oneself
pick up on the fine qualities of others and mimic them,
later they will appear, you will encounter them,
the ideas that do not leave with light or with song,
the ideas unmoved by wind or by weather,
and what I have hoped was justice was at times fear,
what I have hoped was friendship was at times friendship,
but I couldn't believe it.
The pool and the light reflecting off it.
The pool and us swimming below it.
It is not the same water cycling through the spring,
though it feels the same.
We live for recognition and the failures of recognition
and such attendance gives us strength.
The placement of ink on cloth or that dust
which does pile in light of our superiority.

I have come to you with my wants
and so you have seen my wants.
A delicate treatment.
A fragile investment.

There are those who smartly save their resources
and then there is time.
How softly a pigeon may land on the concrete,
and how terrible is a terrible dream.
In your office I tried to explain it,
but we are entering a century of explanations and offers
and I hoped to provide for you a respite from such strains,
a walk through the pines with friends,
not elucidation,
but a peck on the cheek of the mechanism that got us here,
not an empty sound bounced off a window
but the perfect execution of elevation
like hats taken off in habit,
like some actual people pushing through the pines
which easily you might read as us the sun or the real.
Read the forest.
Speak of the trees.
Understand what allows the canopy to be.
Ives in want of rain
and the coming across of puddles, light,
and let me lean over you and show you this
which I have spread out before you:

      here, the nonsensical esplanade
      here, an intertwining circle of daisies
      here, the beautiful guest house to which we will repair

(it is a cottage really) in the oldest fashion,

---

crooked, stone and unabashed in the presence of dew,
a world has grown around it with the graceful living and dying
of flora in exaggerated patterns constantly noted.
Ability will creep up on one, and carefulness as well.
I wanted to break the dish so I could be sorry
for having done it.
The dish holds the candy,
the candy holds the sugar,
and the sweetness of our people is gone
and in its place aloofness, ridicule and
a distant whisper we try to remember.
On sea set sail.
On land sit still.
Contrive a windy mutuality if you must
but the pills will only make you pleasant to yourself –
and what is to follow is but weather and circumstance.
The day speaks of the night and the night speaks of the day
and always clouds elevate themselves into translucency.
Somewhere a willow sways above a pool.
Here is the pool.
Here is where the willow will go.